Alice Beyer

"By the grace God has given me, I laid a foundation as a wise builder, and someone else is building on it. But each one should build with care. For no one can lay any foundation other than the one already laid, which is Jesus Christ."

(1 Corinthians 3:10 & 11)

Is This My Father's House?
© 2011 Alice Beyer

ISBN 978-1-937514-10-5

Printed in the United States of America

Published in association with
    Camden House Books, LLC
    10026-A South Mingo Road, Suite 291
    Tulsa, Oklahoma 74133

Dedication

I dedicate this book to Edward Beyer, my loving husband of thirty-eight years, to my best friend and my encourager, a man who has a heart for God. Thank you for your patience and love. I'll love you forever—from the ceiling to the floor.

With much love and pride, I dedicate this book to Eddie, Michelle, and David, my children, who are a gift from God; and to my daughters-in-law, Marla and Lindsey. Thank you for your love and encouragement to keep on keeping on. You have given me so much love and joy. I'll love you forever—from the ceiling to the floor.

To our precious grandchildren, I dedicate this book to Moriah, Declan, Hannah, and Jude Kingsley, who have brought so much joy and love into our lives. I did not know there was such a love!

With gratitude, I thank my pastors, Andrew Surace, Pete Whipple, Bud Smith, and Dennis and Denny Postell, who patiently answered many of my questions and invested their lives into mine.

I would like to thank the Gospel Crusade Ministerial Association and my overseer, Pastor Ron Bauza, for his encouragement and for believing in me.

Most of all, I dedicate this book to my Lord and Savior, Jesus Christ:

Thank You for Your grace that You have poured out on my life.

Thank you for Your faithfulness and mercy each and every day.

Thank You for the privilege to meet with You daily and hear Your voice.

Acknowledgments

I would like to thank the Holy Spirit for directing me to Dr. Larry Keefauver for his help and advice in the publishing of *Is This My Father's House?* devotional.

It is a blessing to honor Pam McLaughlin, who was introduced into my life to help edit the work God asked me to do. Her God-given gifts, talents, and insight are truly being used for His glory.

She helped to bring this devotional from the pregnancy stage into the birthing stage for the Lord Jesus' Body to be able to have some insights into the heart of God.

With a grateful heart, I thank our son, David, and Blake Vasek for using their creativity and gifts to design the cover for *Is This My Father's House?*

I would also like to thank David Hail for his insight, patience, and prayful support. It has been a delight and honor working with him.

*I will stand at my watch and station myself
on the ramparts;
I will look to see what he will say to me,
and what answer I am to give to this complaint.
Then the LORD replied:
"Write down the revelation and make
it plain on tablets
so that a herald may run with it.
For the revelation awaits an appointed time;
it speaks of the end and will not prove false.
Though it linger, wait for it; it will certainly come
and will not delay."*
(Habakkuk 2:1 – 3 NIV)

As you meditate on the following pages, open up your heart to the Spirit of God and see what He is saying to you personally. Our heart is to impart golden nuggets into your life. So it is by the grace of God these words are penned.

But by the Grace of God I am what I am.
(1 Corinthians 15:10)

Table of Contents

Introduction
My House Will Be Called a House
of Prayer xi

Day One
Can You See the Rain? 17

Day Two
Are You Lonely? 21

Day Three
Would I Be Found Naked? 25

Day Four
Get Ready! 29

Day Five
I Have Given You a Book 33

Day Six
Is That You, Lord? 37

Day Seven
Let the Labor Pains Begin! 41

Day Eight
Do You Hear the Alarm? 45

Day Nine
Just Off a Little Bit 51

Day Ten
All We Need Is Love 55

Day Eleven
May I Be Found Faithful 59

Day Twelve
My Body Hurts 65

Day Thirteen
Suddenly the Wind Came 69

Day Fourteen
Are You Here to Worship Me? 73

Day Fifteen
Looking in but Never Entering 79

Day Sixteen
Can You Hear the Voice? 85

Day Seventeen
This Is Not a Guessing Game 89

Day Eighteen
I Could Use a Little Windex 95

Day Nineteen
Open My Eyes, Lord 99

Day Twenty
It's Time to Be Quiet 103

Day Twenty-One
Do You Trust Me? 109

Day Twenty-Two
  Do You Only Want a Visitation? 115

Day Twenty-Three
  How Did It Get So Complicated?..................119

Day Twenty-Four
  Where Is My GPS?..................123

Day Twenty-Five
  Not Even a Hint..................129

Day Twenty-Six
  What a Wonder..................133

Day Twenty-Seven
  Could I Be the One?..................137

Day Twenty-Eight
  Now That's a LOT of LOVING!..................141

Day Twenty-Nine
  Magnets—the Power to Draw!..................145

Day Thirty
  Wait for the Gift..................149

Conclusion
  The Free Gift of God..................159

About the Author..................163

Introduction

My House Will Be Called a House of Prayer

Did you ever go to a concert? You paid mega-bucks to see the main attraction. Your excitement starts way before you even begin your day. You plan your trip early so you can be first in line. You just can't wait for the performer to come on stage!

Finally, it is getting closer for the curtain to be drawn. Suddenly, out comes the "pre-entertainment." Not one or two, but three up-and-coming artists just wanting a chance to show everyone who they are and what they can do. It feels like you have been there for hours and you haven't even seen who you came for. It's getting later and later and everyone is getting antsy.

Somehow this entire thought came to my mind as the Holy Spirit opened my eyes to see how we come before God. When we come together for our

Sunday Celebration, do we come with excitement? Are we coming just to a concert or a show? Do we ever get to the main attraction?

Look with me in Matthew 21:12-13 when Jesus arrives at the Temple.

> *Jesus entered the temple area and drove out all who were buying and selling there. He overturned the tables of the money changers and the benches of those selling doves. "It is written," He said to them, "'My house will be called a house of prayer,' but you are making it 'a den of robbers.'"*

Again in Mark 11:17 we read, "And as he taught them, he said, 'Is it not written: *My house will be called a house of prayer* for all nations"? But you have made it 'a den of robbers.'"

As we were concluding our teachings on foundational truths, the Holy Spirit spoke to my heart: *"There is still one more thing that is missing in My House—PRAYER."* Notice with me the word He said here: "MISSING! In His House!"

I had the privilege to watch a sermon that was recorded at the Praise Gathering, "My House Shall Be Called a House of Prayer," by Pastor Jim Cymbala, and my heart was pierced. Over and over he emphasized that "prayer" must be the main priority in the spiritual life of each individual and in the life of the Church.

Does it seem we have a tendency to do everything else? Many times we have our mini concert of praise, our relevant message, and little time is given to our God in prayer. Did we have a real encounter with the Lord? Did we come to His throne of grace? May I be so bold as to say, did we get to the main attraction yet?

Let us then approach (God's) throne of grace with confidence, so that we may receive mercy and find grace to help us in our time of need.
(Hebrews 4:16 NIV)

Read this prayer out loud as you begin your journey through this collection of Daily Reflections:

Dear Father, please forgive me for being so distracted that I would neglect my time of prayer—that I have prayer among the least of my priorities. Even as the disciples asked You to teach them to pray, may I humble myself to seek You and Your ways in prayer. Make me a house of prayer. Thank You that You have chosen prayer as a way for You to impart Your wisdom and blessings into my life. Amen

 ## Time to Get Your Hiking Boots On

Have you ever been in a situation where someone asked you to help them and you find yourself doing the entire project yourself? I see that in the spirit realm as well. It seems easier to have someone else do all the praying, seeking God and studying the Word of God, then just share what they have learned. It seems it has been this way for a long time.

When the people saw the thunder and lightning and heard the trumpet and saw the mountain in smoke, they trembled with fear. They stayed at a distance and said to Moses, "Speak to us yourself and we will listen. But do not have God speak to us or we will die." Moses said to the people, "Do not be afraid. God has come to test you, so that the fear of God will be with you to keep you from sinning." The people remained at a distance, while Moses approached the thick darkness where God was. (Exodus 20:18-21 NIV)

Moses chose to draw near to God and seek Him face-to-face, but the Israelites were satisfied to know Him at a distance. "Go near and listen to all that the LORD our God says. Then tell us whatever the LORD our God tells you. We will listen and obey" (Deuteronomy 5:27 NIV).

The Lord spoke to my heart: *"You cannot manufacture My presence."* It takes time and work to build a relationship with God, but it is well worth it. God is looking for us to get our "hiking boots" on, climb that mountain, and seek Him for ourselves. He desires to spend time with us—He is patiently waiting!

To help you get started with the process of building a relationship with God, I will include opportunities for you to ***get your hiking boots on*** all throughout this book. If you will take the responsibility for learning what God has to say for yourself, you will be richly rewarded by your heavenly Father. He so desires to "open the floodgates of heaven and pour out so much blessing that you will not have room for it" (Malachi 3:10b).

Day One

Can You See the Rain?

It is so precious when the Holy Spirit speaks to your very heart. Never take it for granted or close your ear to His voice. In John 16:13 Jesus said, "But when He, the Spirit of truth, comes, He will guide you into all truth. He will not speak on His own; He will speak only what He hears, and He will tell you what is to come" (NIV).

During a time of worship, the gentle voice of His Spirit spoke to my heart, *"Recognize the urgency of the times."*

Immediately, my mind remembered the following Scripture:

He said to the crowd: "When you see a cloud rising in the west, immediately you say, 'It's going to rain,' and it does. And when the south wind blows, you say, 'It's going to be hot,' and

*it is. Hypocrites! You know how to interpret
the appearance of the earth and the sky. How
is it that you don't know how to interpret this
present time?"* (Luke 12:54-56 NIV)

How do we learn to interpret this present time?
Once again, the voice of the Holy Spirit spoke,
"Bring My people back to Me."

The God of the universe, the Creator of all things,
desires to be with you and me! He loves us so much
He wants to spend time with us, talk to us, instruct
and guide us. Can you even begin to image how awesome that is? He waits for us to take the time to meet
together with Him. How can we be too busy for God?

At times I wonder, "Why do I procrastinate
before I come to Him?"

I love my time with the Lord, His gentle smile,
and His love that I feel radiates to me. I think of how
faithful God is and how He met with Adam and Eve
in the Garden. Even when they hid, He called out
to them to let them know He was there waiting and
looking for them.

Today He still calls out to me and to you and He
waits for us to make time for Him. We need to begin
to realize just how precious our time together with
God is for us and for Him.

*And I will give them a heart to know me, that
I am the LORD: and they shall be my people,
and I will be their God: for they shall return
unto me with their whole heart.*
(Jeremiah 24:7 KJV)

 ## Time to Get Your Hiking Boots On

Read John 16:5-15. Why did Jesus tell His disciples that it was good that He return to the Father in heaven? _____

_____

How did Jesus describe the Holy Spirit? _____

_____

What do you think is the best way to find out what pleases God? _____

Read Jeremiah 24:7. What does this Scripture say God wants from His people? _____

If we do what He asks us to do in this Scripture, what does He promise us? _____

Pray this prayer out loud from your heart:

> *Thank You Lord, for calling to me, for looking and waiting for us to be together. May I draw closer to You, my Lord, and cherish our sweet fellowship together. Let me not let the business of the day keep me from You. I know Lord, that if I spend time with You and take time to listen, You will direct my day to be effective and bring You glory.*

Day Two

Are You Lonely?

After setting up the room for the children for Sunday Church, I stepped into the sanctuary. It was dark and quiet. I took one deep breath and gently let it out. Suddenly, a sense of stillness came over me, and then a sobering feeling of loneliness. The presence of God filled the room, and yet this feeling of loneliness was still there. I could not move to leave. Seconds went by as I tried to understand what I was feeling.

Suddenly, I found myself asking God, "Are You lonely?"

His surprising response to me was, *"My kids keep Me busy."*

My immediate response was, "Yes, but are You lonely?"

My heart broke as His response remained the same and my heart began to weep. How can the

Creator of the heavens and earth be lonely? How can Almighty God be lonely? And yet such an awakening of this emotion flooded my very being.

Have you ever been in a crowded room, with friends or even with family, and still felt you were alone? You could even be the life of the party, laughing and joking, yet find yourself overcome by a deep sense of loneliness. The pain is nearly unbearable!

God has promised us that as His beloved children, we are never alone. Our God is always with us; He will never leave us or forsake us (Joshua 1:5). Yet, at times we can leave Him and forsake Him. His love will always be there for us no matter what our circumstances. He will be there waiting for us to once again reach out for His hand with a heart of repentance.

Then the man and his wife heard the sound of the LORD God as he was walking in the garden in the cool of the day, and they hid from the LORD God among the trees of the garden. (Genesis 3:8 NIV)

 ## Time to Get Your Hiking Boots On

In Joshua 1:5 and again in Hebrews 13:5, God promises us _____

Psalm 27:10 tells us that even if our loved ones forsake us, _____

If you are like me, you may have been a little critical of the behavior of the disciples in Matthew Chapter 26 when Jesus was praying in Gethsemane and at the time of His arrest. But how many times have we fallen asleep while praying? How many times have we been too busy or too tired to give Him more than a few minutes at the start or close of our day? Isn't that forsaking Him? _____

Read Luke 11:10. What does God promise us if we seek to find Him? _____

Read the Parable of the Prodigal Son in Luke 15:11-24. We are often like the prodigal son. However, God is like the boy's father in the story. What does verse 20 say about the father? What did the father do when the son returned to him? (see verse 22-24)

_____
_____
_____

Sincerely pray this prayer:

Lord, forgive me for contributing to Your loneliness. May I never again ignore You and cause You such pain. Draw me each day into Your presence for sweet fellowship.

Day Three

Would I Be Found Naked?

So I prophesied as he commanded me, and breath entered them; they came to life and stood up on their feet—a vast army.

(Ezekiel 37:10 NIV)

Shortly after our move to Florida, I was sitting on my comfy couch spending time with my Lord. The Holy Spirit allowed me to see a vision of a vast army that stretched as far as my eyes could see. Standing before everyone was the Lord. I noticed that some of those approaching the Lord were dressed and some were not. The Lord would hand orders to those that were dressed and directed them to stand at His right. Those who were not dressed were told to stand to His left.

I heard the Spirit of the Lord say, *"I will come one more time to My people to prepare them, one more time, if they listen, they listen."*

This sobering feeling came upon me that God was grieving that there were those among His Body that were not prepared to go to battle. I felt in my spirit that God was drawing His people together, setting apart those He would send out as His Army. It was time for me to search my own heart and see if I was preparing myself, or would I be found naked?

"Be dressed ready for service and keep your lamps burning, like men waiting for their master to return from a wedding banquet, so that when he comes and knocks they can immediately open the door for him. It will be good for those servants whose master finds them watching when he comes. I tell you the truth, he will dress himself to serve, will have them recline at the table and will come and wait on them." (Luke 12:35 NIV)

 ## Time to Get Your Hiking Boots On

When you are in a military boot camp, everything is stripped from you. It is a time of breaking until you only listen to the voice of your commander. God is trying to break us and humble us so we will be ready to hear Him when He sends out the call.

Read 2 Timothy 2:3-4.

What advice did Paul give to Timothy in these verses? _____

How does that apply to us as we prepare to join the Army of the Lord? _____

What changes do you need to make in your life so that you will not be found naked when the call to battle is given? _____
_____

God wants us to come to life, take a stand, and be an active member of His Army. We need to be so connected to Him that we clearly hear His voice.

Sincerely pray this prayer:

> *I cry out to you, O Lord; cover my naked-*
> *ness with Your grace and mercy. Forgive me*
> *for going my own way and not seeking Your*
> *heart. Search me, my Lord; open my heart to*
> *Yours. May my heart beat as Your heart beats,*
> *that I may be humbled before You. My desire*
> *is to honor You in obedience to Your will.*

Day Four

Get Ready!

It was a Tuesday morning and the ladies were coming together for a time of prayer. During this time, I felt to lay prostrate on the floor as I prayed. In the Spirit I saw two fields; both were ripe for harvest. The first field was the field of the "harvest of the Christians."

"Why would we need to harvest this field?" I asked.

The Spirit spoke to me saying, *"I am trying to get the Body of Christ ready."*

We have become like a young bird content to stay in the nest and wait for momma bird to bring us one more worm to eat. We sit in church with our mouths wide open waiting for the pastor to teach us one more thing and then we will be ready to leave the nest to go do what we have been created to do. As we eagerly anticipate another juicy revelation from the Lord, delivered to us by our spiritual leaders, we sit week after week totally unaware of what is going on all around us. The field is so very ripe for the harvest, yet we feel we are not ready to go participate in the harvest.

The second field was of course the field of the "harvest of the lost."

Recently I saw the same vision again, except this time the one field of the harvest of Christians was beginning to disappear, leaving the field of the lost as the very prominent one. It was then I realized that our time to get ready was coming to an end.

> *"My food," said Jesus, "is to do the will of Him who sent me and to finish his work. Do you not say, 'Four months more and then the harvest?' I tell you, open your eyes and look at the fields! They are ripe for harvest. Even now the reaper draws his wages; even now he harvests the crop for eternal life, so that the sower and the reaper may be glad together."*
> (John 4:34-36 NIV)

You see, this season will come to an end and it will be no more. Just like when a cornfield is already white for harvest. It is already past due and is about to go bad, about to spoil. Are we ready to witness to others and tell them our story of how Jesus has changed our life, or will we remain lethargic and continue letting these opportunities pass us by? I believe the Lord is warning us it is time to get ready!

 ## Time to Get Your Hiking Boots On

The Lord Jesus was most adamant about preparing His disciples to continue His work once it was time for Him to return to the Father. Each one of the Gospels gives an account of how Jesus warned His followers to be aware of the seasons.

Read Matthew 9:35-38. What did Jesus tell His disciples to pray for? _____

Read Mark 4:26-29. What was Jesus teaching concerning the harvest in this passage? _____

_____

_____

Read Luke 9:62-10:2. What did Jesus tell His disciples to pray and do? _____

_____

_____

Read John 4:34-38. What is the Lord revealing to you in this passage? _____

_____

_____

31

Sincerely pray this prayer out loud:

Lord of the harvest, hear my prayer. Please help me to have eyes to see and ears to hear Your voice and Your directions. May You have confidence in me that I will not let this field die and spoil. Help me to seek You in all things first and have Your heart for the lost.

Day Five

I Have Given You a Book

"My ears had heard of you, but now my eyes have seen you."   (Job 42:5 NIV)

Did you ever notice how everyone has a book for you to read? When I began to develop my relationship with Jesus Christ, it seemed everyone had something I just had to read. It became very overwhelming to me. How could I possibly read all the books that well-intentioned people recommended to me? How would I ever understand what a true relationship with Jesus Christ really was like?

The calming whisper of God spoke to my anxious spirit saying, *"I have given you a book, My Word. Know My Word first and then you will be able to discern the relevance of the other books."*

What liberation! I needed the solid foundation of God's Word hidden in my heart so that I would not sin against Him. His Word speaks to my heart each day, giving me instruction and direction. As I diligently search His Word, He shows me His amazing grace and unmerited mercy. He willingly gives me understanding as I read the Words He has penned and made available to His children.

 ## Time to Get Your Hiking Boots On

Read 2 Peter 1:2-4. What has our loving heavenly Father given us so that we can participate in His divine nature and escape the corruption of the world? _____

Read 2 Peter 1:5-8. What are we to do so that we will not be ineffective or unproductive in our Christian walk? _____

_____

_____

_____

Your heavenly Father is just waiting to open up His amazing truths to you. All you need to do is take the time to read the beautiful letters He has written to you as His beloved child.

Read James 1:16-18. What truth did you receive from this passage of His Word? _____

_____

_____

Take the time to thank God today for His most precious Words to you.

Thank You, gracious God, for coming to me in my time of need. May I always meditate on Your Word and keep it in my heart that I may not sin against You. Thank you for these Words that bring me life.

Day Six

Is That You, Lord?

Every word of God is pure; He is a shield to those who put their trust in Him. Do not add to His words, lest He rebuke you, and you be found a liar. (Proverbs 30:5-6 NKJV)

You hear so many words today that start with, "Thus says the Lord…" Honestly, some are so obviously not from the Lord that you wonder if the one speaking even knows the Word of God at all. Then there are some that have some truth mixed in them but are not the whole truth.

After the Lord had said these things to Job, he said to Eliphaz the Temanite, "I am angry with you and your two friends, because you have not spoken of me what is right, as my servant Job has." (Job 42:7 NIV)

When we read the Scriptures concerning Job and the counsel of his friends, we see that God was angry with them because they incorrectly represented His ways. The Church should be a reflection of the character of God. We should look the same and sound the same!

I was truly sad the day I heard the Spirit of the Lord speak to my heart concerning a so-called word from the Lord, *"I haven't even put My initials on that, let alone My signature."*

Do you have a standard for judging what you hear proclaimed as truth? There is only one way to know for sure. It must not contradict the written WORD of God.

 ## Time to Get Your Hiking Boots On

Read 2 Timothy 2:15. What instructions are we given concerning the Word of God? _____

_____

_____

How are we to be obedient to these instructions?

_____

Read Hebrews 4:12-13. Why is it so important that we correctly handle the Word of God? _____

_____

_____

Read Colossians 3:16. All that we say and do should be based on what? _____

Will you pray this prayer with a sincere and grateful heart?

Father, may I never add to Your Word or misrepresent You in any way. Let my life be a reflection of You in all that I do. May You give me the spirit of wisdom and revelation and enlighten the eyes of my understanding.

Day Seven

Let the Labor Pains Begin!

"I will birth in you a new compassion for the hurting and a desire for Me. As you grow, there will be times of discomfort and even labor pains, but the birth will be worth it. Let Me strengthen you. There is a time of preparing. I am looking for a people who will come with clean hands and a pure heart. I am looking for a people who will move forward and not lag behind; the waters have been still too long. I am looking for a people who will be obedient to the voice of the Lord. Clothe yourself for battle; get rid of all anger, lust, and greed; for they have no place in My house."

(Word of the Lord)

We are called to represent God to the world around us. So, I would say that means He wants us to reflect who He is and act like Him. Think with me a minute. A pregnant woman has nine months of preparing for the birth of her baby. As the time of the child's birth approaches, there is growth, discomfort, and then the day arrives when the labor pains begin. There is no new birth without the labor pains. The birth of a new child truly reflects the awesomeness of God to me.

Our God, our Father, is looking for His children to be obedient to His voice, to have His heart and His character. Yes, there will be times we will experience growing pains, stretching and learning to be obedient to the Word of God. We must never lose heart even when we are in the midst of the labor pains. We need to constantly remind ourselves we have been created in His image! Let us strive to get rid of everything that entangles us and causes us to stumble and fall as we keep our eyes on the Author and Finisher of our faith.

Therefore, since we are surrounded by such a great cloud of witnesses, let us throw off everything that hinders and the sin that so easily entangles. And let us run with perseverance the race marked out for us, fixing our eyes on Jesus, the pioneer and perfecter of faith. For the joy set before him endured the cross, scorning its shame, and sat down at the right hand of the throne of God. Consider him who endured such opposition from sinful men, so that you will not grow weary and lose heart. (Hebrews 12:1-3 NIV)

 ## Time to Get Your Hiking Boots On

Hebrews 12:1-3 gives us some very specific things to do in order to be that true reflection of God that He desires for each of us to be.

Verse 1 lists three things we are to do:

   1- We are to throw off _____

      _____

   2- We are to disentangle ourselves from _____

      _____

   3- We are to _____ with _____
      the race He has marked out for us.

Verse 2 continues the list but also tells us why we must do this all important step.

   1- We are to fix our eyes on _____

   2- Because He is the _____ and
      _____ of our faith.

   3- He set the example for us by _____
      the cross and shame.

4- So that we will not grow _____
    or _____ heart.

As you think about what it means to be God's true
representative, spend some time in prayer.

*Father, in Your Word You ask us to get rid of
all bitterness and anger, and to be kind and
compassionate to one another. You tell us we
are to be forgiving to each other, just as You
have forgiven us. Help me to be that reflection
of You in all that I say and do. Father God,
may we be one as You and the Son are one.*

Day Eight

Do You Hear the Alarm?

Satan, he who is the seducer (deceiver) of all humanity the world over...

(Revelation 12:9 AMP)

The Holy Spirit gave me a vision one night at a youth group service that caused me to weep and pray:

> *I saw flames that were reaching toward our children and young adults. I heard horrid laughing and saw Satan dancing a victory dance as he declared, "I have put upon them a spirit of deception so they cannot discern good from evil. They are becoming disillusioned as to what the Word of God says. I have put blinders on them so they can no longer discern what is truth and what is a lie."*

The world is already deceived...they know not the truth. Now the enemy is focusing on our "church kids." I asked the Holy Spirit to confirm with Scripture what I had seen and asked for wisdom to test and see if the vision was of the Lord. The Scripture began to confirm the vision:

The Holy Spirit clearly says that in later times some will abandon the faith and follow deceiving spirits and things taught by demons.
(1 Timothy 4:1 NIV)

One night our house alarm went off and I jumped up to see what was going on. I had forgotten that because of some minor eye surgery I had a patch over one eye and a breathing mask on. The intruder only took one quick look and then screamed at my distorted shadow as I came around the corner. I think I screamed as well! At that particular moment, I am not sure who was more scared. Fortunately, it scared the intruder off, but the Lord used that situation to show me something in the spirit realm.

"There is an alarm going off in the heavens because an intruder has come into our midst, because our vision has become distorted and we have become dull of hearing."

Satan wants to distort our vision and cause distraction so we cannot hear the voice of God. Then he can pervert the Word of the Lord the same way he did in the Garden with Eve. He deceived her into taking her eyes off of what God had freely given her and pointed out what she could not have. He distorted God's character and cleverly misquoted what God had really said. The enemy employs this same tactic with God's people today. His goal is to distort the truth and draw us away from our loving heavenly Father.

1 Peter 5:8 warns us to, "Be self-controlled and alert. Your enemy the devil prowls around like a roaring lion looking for someone to devour" (NIV).

We read in Acts 20:29-31a, "I know after I leave, savage wolves will come in among you and will not spare the flock. Even from your own number men will arise and distort the truth in order to draw away disciples after them. So be on your guard" (NIV).

 ## Time to Get Your Hiking Boots On

One thing we must remember, Jesus Christ has not changed His message to accommodate the changing times. His words are as relevant today as they were when He walked this earth.

Read Hebrews 13:8-9.

What does it tell us about Jesus Christ? _____

_____

Verse 9 says the reason we need to remember this is so we will not be _____

_____

_____

Read 2 Corinthians 11:3-4.

The writer was afraid that the followers of Jesus might be what? _____

What did he warn the believers to watch out for?

_____

Read 2 Corinthians 11:14-15.

Satan masquerades as what? _____

_____

Satan's servants masquerade as what? _____

_____

Read 1 John 4:1-3.

What does this passage tell us to do in order to discern if what we are hearing is from God, the enemy, or the world? _____

_____

You and I do not have to be deceived. Ask the Holy Spirit right now to give you the ability to discern what is of God and what is not:

> *Holy Spirit, I welcome You to come. Help me to be alert and hear the sounds of the alarm. Help me not to be caught off guard. O Lord, help me to be sensitive to Your leading and to know when something is not right or against Your Word. Please release Your discerning gift upon my life.*

Day Nine

Just Off a Little Bit...

By the grace God has given me, I laid a foundation as a wise builder, and someone else is building on it. But each one should build with care. For no one can lay any foundation other than the one already laid, which is Jesus Christ. (1 Corinthians 3:10-11 NIV)

The Spirit of the Lord gave me a vision one day of an extremely tall building. It was beautiful to look at; however, the foundation had cracks and was beginning to crumble. The Lord said to me, *"Take My Church back to the basics, and build its foundation."*

We were building what we called our downsized retirement home. The plans had been finalized by the architect; subcontractors were all lined up, ready to start; and the supplies were being delivered. Almost every day we could go by and just "check things out." After the foundation was laid, the block walls started to go up. We were excited to see it taking shape, but I kept feeling something didn't seem quite right. I couldn't put my finger on it, so the work continued.

The inside began to take on some character, but again, things didn't seem just right. We checked and rechecked the plans, but could find nothing to indicate anything was off track. It wasn't until they started putting in the kitchen counters that we began to understand what was happening. The countertop didn't quite line up, the door to the office was off-center, and the electrical sockets were in the wrong places. The drawing was off by one-quarter of an inch, but that equaled a five-foot difference in the width of the house. It was just off a little bit, but it caused major changes in the overall stability of the structure!

As a homeowner, from time to time you must go over your home to do a little pre-maintenance. This assures you everything is in working order and can save you from a disaster in the future. The same care should also apply to our spiritual buildings. Could it be we are off just a little bit and need to make some repairs?

I am reminded of the story of Isaac and his two sons in Genesis 27. Jacob came to his father and deceived him to gain Esau's blessing for himself. I noticed that four times blind Isaac asked if the son before him was Esau or Jacob. Could it be that Isaac was discerning that it just didn't seem quite right? I wonder how many times we discern that something in our spirit just doesn't seem right but fail to ask the Lord to show us the truth.

 ## Time to Get Your Hiking Boots On

Jesus touched on this subject of the wise and foolish builders.

Read Luke 6:46-49.

What is the foundation that Jesus says we need to build on so our lives can withstand the storms of life? _____

_____

How do we build on a solid foundation? _____

_____

Read James 1:5-8.

What is the promise God gives us in verse 5? _____

_____

Compare verse 6 to the foolish builder.

What causes us to be blown about by the storms of life? _____

What does this say a double-minded man is? _____

_____

53

As you determine to build your spiritual house on the sure foundation of Jesus Christ, pray daily and ask the Lord for a discerning heart and wisdom from above.

Father, I thank You for Your grace that You have given to me so that I may live a life that will be pleasing to You. Please help me to care for my spiritual house and to build upon my foundation in Christ with truth and clarity. Thank You for a discerning heart and for wisdom with understanding. I thank You for Your Word that directs my path.

Day Ten

All We Need Is Love

Jesus replied, "'Love the Lord your God with all your heart and with all your soul, and with all your mind." This is the first and the greatest commandment. And the second is like it: 'Love your neighbor as yourself.'"
(Matthew 22:37-39 NIV)

This Scripture is the foundation of the New Beginnings Ministry. The Holy Spirit gave this Scripture to us as the very foundation of our heart for this ministry. Sounds so simple, and yet it is so profound. Can you imagine loving the Lord with ALL of your heart, with ALL of your soul, and with ALL of your mind? Even as I read this powerful Scripture, I knew deep in my heart I could not stand here and say that I have given ALL of my heart to my precious Lord. My desire is to love Him with everything within me, to love the Lord with ALL. I discovered a very profound truth about the Word of God; when it says "all," it means "ALL!"

The very foundation of this Scripture says to me that ALL my actions, ALL my conversations and ALL my obedience to my Lord would surely be reflected by my love and devotion to Him. Could a human mind even begin to grasp what the world would be like if we all loved God with all of our heart, soul, and mind? Then if we were to take it a step further and loved our neighbors as we loved ourselves, what kind of people we would be? We could turn the world upside down! Our lives would radically change and those around us would surely see the love of God within our hearts. All I can say to this is, "WOW!"

As I meditate on this one small passage of Scripture, I wonder if we would just do these two commandments given to us by the Lord Jesus Himself, maybe we wouldn't need so many "How To…" conferences. What do you think?

 **Time to Get Your Hiking Boots On**

Love is such an important and yet controversial subject, even among Christians. The Bible talks about three kinds of love, but the greatest is the God kind of love which is unconditional.

Read 1 John 3:1. God's love for us is so great that He calls us _____!

Read 1 John 4:16. God is _____. Whoever lives in _____ lives in God, and God in him.

Read 1 John 4:19. We love because _____ _____.

Read John 3:16. How would you describe God's love for us? _____

Ask God to further reveal His perfect love to you and then through you.

Father God, may my heart be totally Yours. May I die to myself that I may be able to love You with my entire being. Father, may Your perfect love flow from me to all those around me and bring glory to Your name.

Day Eleven

May I Be Found Faithful

Have you ever been reading the Scriptures when suddenly the words just came so alive to you? This very thing happened to me. I was reading Ezekiel 40:4 when the Lord spoke to my heart that this word was for me.

> *"Look with your eyes and hear with your ears and pay attention to everything I am going to show you, for that is why you have been brought here. Tell the house of Israel every-thing you see."* (Ezekiel 40:4 NIV)

My first impression was, I am going to Israel. God is sending me to Israel. I was ready to start packing my bags! Well, I haven't gotten there yet. But as I settled down and allowed the Lord to bring clarity to what He was showing me, He took me to Jeremiah 15:19.

Therefore this is what the LORD says: "If you repent, I will restore you that you may serve me; if you utter worthy, not worthless, words, you will be my spokesman." (NIV)

You see, I had been so busy doing the ministry of the Lord that I neglected the Lord of the ministry! I found we can be doing all kinds of good things for God and still be disobedient to His voice. When I stopped long enough to seek His direction, He whispered one more correction to my spirit, "I have called you to be a spokesman, and you are running all around doing the campaigning."

In Matthew 25:14-30, Jesus uses a parable to teach us about the gifts and talents we are each given by God. These gifts are given according to the ability God knows we have within us. Not one of us is insignificant in the Kingdom of God. However, we must be faithful to use what we have been given. We must guard our hearts not to be tempted to look at someone else's abilities and covet what they have.

When we say things like, "I wish I could sing like her or preach like him," we are implying God has not given us the right gift or talent. Would you want to stand before God and tell Him you didn't use the gift or talent He gave you because He made a mistake with you? He is the One who has put each one of us within His Body right where He wants us.

He expects us to work together with the other parts to do His will.

When we are faithful to use what He has entrusted to us, we will hear our Master say, "Well done, good and faithful servant! You have been faithful with a few things; I will put you in charge of many things. Come and share your master's happiness!" (Matthew 25:23 NIV).

 ## Time to Get Your Hiking Boots On

Read the Parable of the Talents in Matthew 25:14-30. What did the Master give the first servant? _____

_____

What did the servant do with what he was given?

_____

What was the Master's response to this servant?

_____

What did the second servant receive from the Master? _____

How did he use the talents that were given to him?

_____

How did the Master respond to this servant? _____

_____

What did you learn from the actions and response of the Master to the third servant? _____

_____

_____

I pray you desire to use the talents God has given you so that when He asks you for an accounting, He will be pleased with what you have done and say to you, "Well done good and faithful servant!"

Thank you Lord, for entrusting me with abilities, gifts, and callings to do Your will here on earth. Thank You that it is not by my own strength, but by Your Holy Spirit, who will guide and lead me. May my desire always be to do the work You have called me to do and to please You in all that I say and do.

Day Twelve

My Body Hurts

Did you ever have a knot in your stomach and just start to cry? When this happened to me, I didn't know why, but I didn't like it. As I prayed I felt the Lord speaking to my heart, *"The Body has been wounded and is bleeding; the Body is suffering. You are grieving and so am I."*

When one in the Body suffers, we all should feel the suffering; on the other hand, when one is rejoicing, we too should be rejoicing.

But in fact God has arranged the parts in the body, every one of them, just as he wanted them to be. If they were all one part, where would the body be? As it is, there are many parts, but one body. The eye cannot say to the hand, "I don't need you!" And the head cannot say to the feet, "I don't need you!"

*On the contrary, those parts of the body that
seem to be weaker are indispensable, and
the parts that we think are less honorable we
treat with special honor. And the parts that
are unpresentable are treated with special
modesty, while our presentable parts need no
special treatment. But God has put the body
together, giving greater honor to the parts
that lacked it, so that there should be no division in the body, but that its parts should have
equal concern for each other. If one part suffers, every part suffers with it; if one part is
honored, every part rejoices with it.*"
(1 Corinthians 12:18-26 NIV)

When we come against each other in the Body of
Christ, we are coming against Christ as well. So, if I
tear down one of my brothers or sisters, I would be
coming against Christ. Maybe it's time to realize what
our words and actions are doing to the Body of Christ.

When we look at John 17:22-23 we see how Jesus
prayed for us, "That they may be one as We are one: I
in them and You in Me. May they be brought to com-
plete unity to let the world know that You sent Me and
have loved them even as You have loved Me" (NIV).

Can we even imagine that we could be one as
the Father and the Son are one? Jesus prayed this so
that we would be in unity in His Body and the world
would know that our heavenly Father loves them so
much that He sent His only Son to come to this earth
to give His life so that we all would have eternal life
with Him.

 **Time to Get Your Hiking Boots On**

Read again 1 Corinthians 12:24-27.

Why did God put the members of the Body together?

_____

_____

_____

What does verse 27 say about each of us? _____

_____

Read Romans 12:15-18.

How is this message similar to 1 Corinthians 12:24-27? _____

What does the word "harmony" mean? _____

_____

Read John 17:22-23.

Why did Jesus want us to be one as He and the Father are one? _____

_____

_____

If, like me, you feel you have not been doing your best to bring harmony and unity to the Body of Christ, pray this prayer:

Thank you, Father, for sending Your precious Holy Spirit to dwell within me. My prayer is that I may walk in unity in the Body of Christ and to be mindful of my attitude toward my family and church family. Help me to live in harmony with them and not bring them down. May my words be uplifting and the meditation of my heart be pleasing to You, my God.

Day Thirteen

Suddenly the Wind Came...

"I am a consuming God. I will burn up the hay and stubble and will restore lives that have been oppressed and depressed. There will be a time of shaking to loose that which has been bound. Many will be set free. There will be a sweet fragrance of deliverance that will come." (The Word of the Lord)

Our Lord desires for us to be free in Him. It is by His Holy Spirit, who searches our hearts and brings us to a time of repentance, that we can truly attain a change of heart and move forward in the direction He has chosen for us to go. In the spirit, I saw a boiling pot that brought all the impurities to the surface, and then "suddenly" the wind of the Holy Spirit came and gently blew them all away.

Since we have these promises, dear friends, let us purify ourselves from everything that contaminates body and spirit, perfecting holiness out of reverence for God.
(2 Corinthians 7:1 NIV)

What is the hay and stubble that needs to be burned up and removed from your life? What areas of your life need the deliverance of the Lord? Yield to Him and receive His sweet deliverance.

Jesus has come to bring us to Himself and set us free. What true freedom! We read the words of Jesus in Luke 4:18-19, "The Spirit of the Lord is on me, because He has anointed me to preach good news to the poor. He has sent me to proclaim freedom for the prisoners and recovery of sight for the blind, to release the oppressed, to proclaim the year of the Lord's favor" (NIV).

 ## Time to Get Your Hiking Boots On

Read 1 Corinthians 3:13-15.

What are the two purposes of the fire in verse 13?

_____

_____

What is the hay and stubble that needs to be burned up and removed from your life? _____

_____

_____

What in your life needs the deliverance of the Lord?

_____

Read 2 Corinthians 7:1.

God has given us promises, but what do we have to do to receive them? _____

Read Hebrews 12:28-29.

When there is a time of shaking, when everything around us seems to be falling apart, where is our only security? _____

_____

_____

If you are ready to allow the Holy Spirit to begin that purifying process in your heart, pray this prayer:

Father, please send Your Holy Spirit and search my heart, search my inner motives and bring all to light by Your grace. Thank you for sending Your Son, Jesus, who has brought me true freedom. Thank You for bringing me the good news and for setting me free by the power of the cross.

Day Fourteen

Are You Here to Worship Me?

The Lord was grieved that he had made man on the earth, and His heart was filled with pain. (Genesis 6:6 NIV)

"*A*re *you here to worship Me or are you here because it is the day of worship?*" These words from the Lord pierced my heart! *"I am not common and will not be treated as such; you cannot pacify Me."*

Our Lord God is grieving over His Body. He has been treated as common and we play church to pacify Him. The same way we give a pacifier to a little baby to distract them, we try to pacify our God by doing part of what He has asked us to do.

"A son honors his father, and a servant his master. If I am a father, where is the honor due me? If I am a master, where is the respect due Me?" says the LORD Almighty.
(Malachi 1:6 NIV)

God was angry with the Israelites and sent the prophet Malachi to warn them that what they thought was their act of worship was actually showing contempt for Him. In Exodus 32, the Israelites thought that they could do their little church thing at the foot of the mountain in the name of YAHWEH and this would pacify the LORD. It seems even today that we have manufactured the presence of God and His Holy Spirit so often that we don't know when His presence is among us.

So many times I hear complaints about the worship service and wonder if we really even want to invite the presence of the Lord into our "church worship" services. If our focus is on acknowledging Him as the Creator of everything and praising Him as the most holy and awesome God, then we would not need to worry about whether the music is too loud or the worship service is too long. We would joyfully harmonize with others in a love song of thanksgiving and praise to our God.

"Yet a time is coming," Jesus told the Samaritan woman at the well, "and has now come when the true worshippers will worship the Father in spirit and truth, for they are the kind of worshipers the Father seeks. God is spirit and His worshipers must worship in spirit and in truth" (John 4:23-24 NIV).

I was in a service and the music was wonderful and the lyrics were ministering to me. I was clapping my hands and even had a little jump in my step.

Suddenly the Lord spoke to me saying, *"Alice, are you ready to worship Me yet?"*

I felt ashamed and began to weep in repentance. A fresh outlook on whom I came to worship overwhelmed me and I began to truly worship my God. I was thankful that God corrected me and opened my eyes to what it meant to worship Him in spirit and in truth.

Therefore, I urge you, brothers, in view of God's mercy, to offer your bodies as living sacrifices, holy and pleasing to God—that is your spiritual act of worship.

(Romans 12:1 NIV)

 ## Time to Get Your Hiking Boots On

"For they are the kind of worshipers the Father seeks."

Read John 4:23-24.

How would you define worship? _____
_____

Does your worship show honor and respect to God?
_____

What does it mean to worship the Father in spirit and in truth? _____
_____

Read Romans 12:1.

What does it mean when it says we are to offer our bodies as a living sacrifice?
_____
_____
_____
_____

As you consider how you have worshipped God, join me in asking God's forgiveness for not making our worship pleasing, honorable, and respectful of Who He is!

Forgive me, Father, for coming before You just because it is the day we come together. May my worship to You be a sweet fragrance and pleasing in Your sight. Holy Spirit, please come and bring me back to a heart of worship and worship through me.

Day Fifteen

Looking in but Never Entering

"Go near and listen to all that the Lord God says. Then tell us whatever the Lord our God tells you. We will listen and obey."

(Deuteronomy 5:27 NIV)

Let me share a vision the Lord gave to me that sheds some light on the interchange the children of Israel had with Moses at the foot of the mountain concerning personal intimacy with God.

Someone was crouched down in the bushes looking inside of a house, first through one window, then another. In the living room people were laughing and enjoying fellowship together in an atmosphere of joy and peace. In the dining room there were more people enjoying a meal together in the same wonderful atmosphere. Just outside the bedroom there was someone with their ear to the closed door listening to the sweet intimacy of the ones in the bedroom.

Have we become so satisfied hearing about someone else's intimacy with God that we do not cultivate our own? Think about the Israelites who were satisfied to stay at a distance and let Moses share his experience. Moses' heart was to see and experience God's glory, to know Him and to know His ways. The Lord God cried out in Deuteronomy 5:29, "Oh, that their hearts would be inclined to fear Me and keep all my commands always, so that it might go well with them and their children forever!" (NIV).

Even as I pondered the vision, the Lord spoke to my heart something so poignant I felt the need to totally detoxify myself from all that I thought intimacy with God meant.

"I am not your prostitute, that you can come to Me to have your needs met and then shun Me when I desire intimacy with you," said the Lord.

The Lord's desire is that we come to Him, draw near to Him, and dine with Him because of our love for Him and His love for us. Could it be that we shy away from such intimacy because of our lifestyle or a lukewarm heart? Adam and Eve were hiding because of their nakedness and sin. Still God sought for them in the cool of the day and called out to them, "Where are you?"

He is calling out to us today, "Where are you?"

My desire is not to run to the Lord only when I have a need, but to just sit with Him in sweet fellowship and love on Him. I want to take that time to praise Him for who He is and all that He has already done. This is the place of intimacy where He will instruct me, comfort me, and guide me in His direction.

 **Time to Get Your Hiking Boots On**

"Call to Me and I will answer you and tell you great and unsearchable things you do not know."　　　　(Jeremiah 33:3 NIV)

Read Jeremiah 32:38-41.

Verse 38 reveals God's heart for His people. He desires that we _____

_____

Verse 39 reveals the level of intimacy God desires to have with us.

What does it mean to have singleness of heart and action? _____

Who will benefit if we cultivate this type of relationship with God? _____

Verse 40 lists three things God will do within this intimate relationship with Him:

　　1- He will make an _____

　　_____

　　2- He will never stop _____

　　_____

3- He will inspire us to _____

_____

Why does He do all of this? _____

_____

Verse 41 defines what His level of intimacy is with us.

He rejoices in _____

_____

If you desire a new level of intimacy with God, make this your personal prayer today:

Lord, I do not want to ever turn my back on You when You call to me. May I embrace our time together and build our relationship together as one. Father, may my love for You grow each second of the day until You have all of me! May my mouth be able to utter these words: I love You, my God, with all my heart, with all my soul, and with all my mind. O dear Lord, may I never just come to You with a "give me" attitude, but one with a grateful and humble heart. May our times together always be cherished as we have sweet fellowship together. When my heart would hear, "Where are you?" may I be able to say, "Here I am, Lord; here I am."

Day Sixteen

Can You Hear the Voice?

"The voice of one crying in the wilderness: 'Prepare the way of the Lord; make His paths straight.'" (Isaiah 40:3 and Matthew 3:3 NKJV)

In the month of October, in the year of the Lord 2005, the Holy Spirit spoke: *"For there comes upon the nation a time of stillness, a time of reverence before Me. For the hour of the Lord is near at hand. Prepare yourself, for before you is the completion of one season and the beginning of another. For nothing is hidden from the eye of the Lord. All that is done in secret will be revealed by the Light."*

He will say, "I have long been silent; yes, I have restrained myself. But now, like a woman in labor, I will cry and groan and pant."
(Isaiah 42:14 NLT)

I felt in my spirit that during this season many will turn to salvation in our Lord. Many more will return to the Lord, while others will grow harder and harder as they refuse to answer His call. This is the time for us to rise up, return to the Lord with all of our heart, and be the light the world so desperately needs to see. The lost will be drawn to the light if we will shine brightly enough for them to be able to distinguish us from the world itself. The day of the Lord will come unexpectedly, and then the season will be no more.

Can you hear the voice of one crying, "Prepare!"?

 **Time to Get Your Hiking Boots On**

Read Matthew 11:15. What did Jesus tell us to do?

_____

Read John 8:47. What did Jesus say about our ability to hear God? _____

Read 2 Timothy 4:1-5. What do we need to do so that we will be prepared in and out of season?

_____

_____

Read Psalm 139:23-24. Will you pray with me?

Dear Father, I know that nothing is hidden from You. Please open my eyes to see what You see. Search me and know my heart, and see if there be any wickedness in me. Lord, please prepare me. May I be pure and holy in Your sight. Thank you for Your grace that empowers me to live my life for You.

Day Seventeen

This Is Not a Guessing Game

"I am about to intervene in the affairs of men on the earth. A visitation from God, for the 'Day of the Lord' is coming, for it is at hand. There will be a time of famine—both spiritual and financial—a financial decline. Many will fall away in despair. Prepare them; equip them so they can stand with the right tools. Take heed; things are not as usual."

(Word of the Lord)

God does not keep us out in left field and guessing what we should do. He has given us His Word to direct us. In Matthew 24:1-35, Jesus told His disciples there would be signs of the end of the age. The Apostle Peter took what Jesus said very seriously and said he would keep on reminding everyone to refer to the Scriptures to attain God's truth. Read 2 Peter 1:12-15. He was right; we all need to be reminded from time to time.

The Holy Spirit is restoring and preparing the Body of Christ to be ready for her Bridegroom. The wedding celebration is not far off. If we need to be restored and prepared in order to be ready for the return of Jesus, we must still be lacking in some areas. We need to diligently seek to know what they are.

I asked the Holy Spirit to open my heart to see some things that I didn't realize were in there. There was a time of weeping and repenting when I saw the pride, the busy work, and misplaced priorities in my life. I found I was not giving God first priority in all things. In His mercy, God showed me the inside of my heart. We can look good on the outside, but He is interested on the inside, too.

God showed me this analogy to help me understand why He is so interested in what is going on in the inner parts of my heart. He showed me a very tall, strong tree. To the eye it appeared that nothing could uproot this tree. Then the Spirit said, *"But look at the inside of the tree; it is empty."* What I saw on the outside did not represent what was going on in the inside at all.

Galatians 2:6 says, "As for those who seemed to be important—whatever they were makes no difference to me; God does not judge by external appearance—those men added nothing to my message" (NIV).

In Colossians 1:10, Paul prays for the Church saying, "And we pray this in order that you may live a life worthy of the Lord and may please Him in every way: bearing fruit in every good work, growing in the knowledge of God" (NIV). The work of the Holy Spirit is to cleanse us from the inside and then God's love will radiate out from us so others will see His reflection in us.

 ## Time to Get Your Hiking Boots On

Jesus taught that we are to be the salt of the earth and a light to the world.

Read Matthew 5:13.

What happens if we no longer function as the salt of the earth? _____

Read Matthew 5:14-16.

Why do we need to let our light shine before men?

_____

Read 2 Corinthians 4:6.

Where does God's light have to be in order for others to see the Christ in us? _____

Read John 8:12.

How do we avoid walking in darkness and remain in the light? _____

Are you willing to let the Holy Spirit do what needs to be done in your heart so that your lamp will never go out and others can see God in you? If your answer is yes, pray this prayer with me:

Oh Lord, search me and know me. If there be any wicked way in me, cleanse me, my Lord, for Your glory. Prepare me that I may be found ready for Your return. As I wait for my beloved to come, show me how to keep the oil of my lamp burning until I see You face-to-face.

Day Eighteen

I Could Use a Little Windex

"When His glory shines in, every speck will be magnified," says the Holy Spirit.

Have you ever noticed how your windows look nice and clean until the sun starts to shine in? You wonder how you could have let them get so dirty. The same thing happens with the furniture. They look nicely dusted until the window shades are up and the sun is shining in on them. Suddenly, it looks like they haven't been dusted in a year!

The Holy Spirit was showing me what God means by spiritual housecleaning. In Luke 12:2-3 Jesus told His disciples, "There is nothing concealed that will not be disclosed, or hidden that will not be made known. What you have said in the dark will be heard in the daylight, and what you have whispered in the ear in the inner rooms will be proclaimed from the roofs" (NIV).

It can look like I have everything together, but if I will allow the Holy Spirit to shine His glory deep inside my heart, He will reveal the "dusty areas" and do the internal cleaning that I need.

"Woe to me!" Isaiah cried. "I am ruined! For I am a man of unclean lips, and I live among a people of unclean lips, and my eyes have seen the King, the LORD Almighty" (Isaiah 6:5 NIV).

As the glory of God falls down upon our lives, every little speck that needs to be removed will become magnified to us and the concealed sins deep in our hearts will come to light. This is how our God pours out His grace upon us to help us live a holy life before Him.

 ## Time to Get Your Hiking Boots On

Read Exodus 34:29-35.

How did Aaron and all of the Israelites know Moses had spoken with the Lord? _____

What happened whenever Moses entered God's presence? _____

Read Psalm 89:15.

What happens to those who walk in the light of God's presence? _____

Read Jude 24-25. Make this your prayer today.

> *To Him who is able to keep (me) from fall-*
> *ing and to present (me) before His glorious*
> *presence without fault and with great joy—to*
> *the only God (my) Savior be glory, majesty,*
> *power and authority, through Jesus Christ*
> *(my) Lord, before all ages, now and forever-*
> *more! Amen.* (NIV)

Day Nineteen

Open My Eyes, Lord

But blessed are your eyes because they see, and your ears because they hear."
(Matthew 13:16 NIV)

As I drove to the office one morning, I asked the Lord to give me His heart and His eyes for the world around me. I suddenly was overwhelmed with tears as the presence of God invaded the atmosphere.

He said to me, *"Alice, if I open your eyes to see what I see, you would never get off your knees."*

What took place in the next split second is indescribable. My mind could not even begin to grasp the darkness and pain I saw. God in His mercy and love knew that only a brief glimpse of what He saw was all that I could possibly bear.

As I thought about what I had seen, I wondered, "Lord, how can You handle all of this?"

I didn't know what to pray or even how to pray, but God has given us His Holy Spirit to guide us, even in our prayers for others.

In the same way, the Spirit helps us in our weakness. We do not know what we ought to pray for, but the Spirit himself intercedes for us with groans that words cannot express. And he who searches our hearts knows the mind of the Spirit, because the Spirit intercedes for God's people in accordance with the will of God. (Romans 8:26-27 NIV)

You would have thought this would have burned in my heart to ever keep before me a focus to intercede for the world and the needs of so many. To my shame, I allowed it to be aborted in my spirit for a season, but the Holy Spirit has faithfully rekindled it within me again and again. With humility, I thank the Lord for His grace and mercy as He patiently develops His character in my life.

The prayer of a righteous man is powerful and effective. (James 5:16b NIV)

 ## Time to Get Your Hiking Boots On

Read Romans 8:19. What is creation eagerly expecting? _____

Read Romans 8:21. What is our mission as the children of God? _____

Read Romans 8:26-27. Who will help direct our prayers so we can begin to fulfill our call?

_____

Read Romans 8:28. Everything God has blessed us with is so we can _____

Are you a child of God? _____ Are you a reflection of your heavenly Father? _____

If you are like me, you know you often fall short of the calling God has placed on your life. If your desire is to allow Him to work in and through you, pray this prayer with me:

Thank You Lord, for Your great understanding and love toward me. Use this vessel, this house that You have purchased with Your precious blood, to see with Your eyes, to pray with Your heart, and to intercede for those who are lost. Holy Spirit, work in and through me so I can fulfill my call as a powerful and effective child of God.

Day Twenty

It's Time to Be Quiet

"You are defensive. I am your defense! Injustice will come, say not a word and see the hand of God." (The Word of the Lord)

Has there ever been a time when you were in a situation and you felt like you just came out of the "twilight zone" and none of it makes any sense? We may go through these situations to see how we will handle pressure and if we will put our trust in God. Some of those whirlwinds just draw us closer to God. Our sensitivity to the Holy Spirit during trials is very important.

Remember how the Lord your God led you all the way in the desert these forty years, to humble you and test you in order to know what was in your heart, whether you would keep his commands. (Deuteronomy 8:2 NIV)

I remember that months before I got hit with a most bizarre situation, the Holy Spirit had already given me warning. I wrote down what I heard in my spirit, put a date on it and put it in my Bible, then basically forgot all about it. I should have used it as my daily bookmarker and kept it ever before me. God was preparing my heart for what was about to take place so that I would glorify Him and He would be lifted up in this upcoming situation.

There are warning signs from God all along life's highway. It would not be a good idea to ignore them.

The hardest thing sometimes is to say nothing when we suffer injustice or persecution! That is when we are to depend on God and remember His written Word. 1 Peter 3:9 warns us, "Do not repay evil with evil or insult with insult. On the contrary, repay evil with blessing, because to this you were called so that you may inherit a blessing" (NIV).

Jesus left us an example of how we are to handle trials along our life's journey. He suffered some of the worst forms of injustice and hurt imaginable, yet He remained silent. One of His apostles betrayed Him, one denied Him, and the priests hurled insult after insult at Him, yet He remained silent. The same Holy Spirit that helped Jesus be a true reflection of the Father's heart even in tribulation is in me. He will help me to be still and silent and let God handle any vengeance needed against my accusers or persecutors.

Honor all people, love the brotherhood, fear God, honor the king. Servants, be submissive to your masters with all respect, not only to those who are good and gentle, but also to those who are unreasonable. For this finds favor, if for the sake of conscience toward God a person bears up under sorrows when suffering unjustly. For what credit is there if, when you sin and are harshly treated, you endure it with patience? But if when you do what is right and suffer for it you patiently endure it, this finds favor with God. For you have been called for this purpose, since Christ also suffered for you, leaving you an example for you to follow in His steps, who committed no sin, nor was any deceit found in His mouth; and while being reviled, He did not revile in return; while suffering, He uttered no threats, but kept entrusting Himself to Him who judges righteously.

(1 Peter 2:13-15 NAS)

 **Time to Get Your Hiking Boots On**

Read 1 Peter 2:13-15.

How are we to handle the ignorant talk of foolish people? _____

Read 1 Peter 2:17.

List the four things this verse tells us to do:

Show _____

Love _____

Fear _____

Honor _____

Read 1 Peter 2:23.

What did Jesus do when He was insulted?

_____

What did He do when He suffered?

_____

Who did He entrust Himself to?

_____

Read Psalm 119:105 and Proverbs 3:5.

Will you pray with me?

> *Thank You, Lord, that You have given me Your Word as a lamp for my feet and a light for my path. Keep me still and quiet before You and settle my spirit that I may trust You in all things.*

Day Twenty-One

Do You Trust Me?

"Do you trust Me?" said the Lord.
"Do you really trust Me?" said the Lord again.

Not a question one really wants to be asked by God, especially when He asks it twice. I know how Peter must have felt when the Lord kept asking him if he truly loved Him.

What else could I say except, "Yes Lord, I trust You."

The Lord said, *"You trust Me to the end of the cliff when your feet are still on the ground, but I am about to take you over the cliff. Trust me."*

Suddenly, my entire world felt like it was upside down. I kept telling myself this can't be God. It just doesn't make a bit of sense at all. Later I realized that I wanted to hold on to the familiar and not even consider the unknown. God was indeed shaking all that needed to be shaken.

It's not foolish to be obedient to the voice of the Lord even when He doesn't give you all of the instructions and details. But you do need to know that it is from Him. When it is, you will sense a deep feeling of peace even when it doesn't make any sense. God may even send you confirmation through another person or event.

While I was attending a woman's conference shortly after the above experience with the Lord, the guest speaker was teaching on Daniel 2:20-23. Verse 21 particularly caught my attention, "He changes times and seasons; He sets up kings and deposes them. He gives wisdom to the wise and knowledge to the discerning" (NIV).

It was like she was talking to my very soul when she said, "You are here for such a time as this—you will not miss a moment of My favor; I am waiting for you. It's time!"

Then to top it off, she pointed her finger at me and said, "Let it go! Moses is dead. Shake the dust off your feet even when it hurts, because it will hold you back."

The speaker could not have known that in our household any time we found ourselves focusing on the things of the past, we would say to one another, "Moses is dead; let it go."

In other words, forget what is behind, stop focusing on it, and get focused on now; forgive and forget. When the speaker said those words, it pierced through my heart. I knew God was confirming His instructions to me so I would separate myself from the current situation, let it go, and trust Him. One of my favorite Scriptures is Proverbs 3:5: "Trust in the LORD with all your heart and lean not on your own understanding; in all your ways acknowledge him, and he will make your paths straight" (NIV).

 **Time to Get Your Hiking Boots On**

Read Daniel 2:1-18.

Where was Daniel working? _____
_____

What position did he hold in Nebuchadnezzar's court? _____

What was going to happen if God didn't answer their prayers? _____

Read Daniel's full song of praise in Daniel 2:20-23.

Was Daniel's trust in God fulfilled? _____

Explain: _____

Read Romans 9:23.

What is the promise given to those who trust in God? _____

Are you willing to ask God to help you be obedient and trust in Him? If your answer is yes, pray:

Lord, You know how my flesh doesn't want to always obey, especially when I don't understand what is going on around me. Teach me how to be obedient to Your will and trust in Your Word.

Day Twenty-Two

Do You Only Want
a Visitation?

*And in Him you too are being built together
to become a dwelling in which God lives by
His Spirit.* (Ephesians 2:22)

One Sunday morning, I stood trembling at the altar, waiting for the pastor to give me a glance. The Holy Spirit had given me a word for the congregation, but I wanted to make sure I honored the pastor and did things in godly order, as the Word of God instructs. He looked over at me, our eyes met, and he knew God wanted me to bring them His Word. He handed me the microphone as I tried to still my racing heart. It felt like I couldn't even breathe, but I had told the Lord I would be obedient to His call and I would trust Him to do the talking.

"You cry out to Me, 'we want a visitation of Your presence, O God, come and visit us.' " The Holy Spirit proclaimed, "I cry out for permanent residency!"

What took place in the next moments could never have happened in a teaching seminar or a conference. In His great mercy and grace, God extended His hand in loving correction and brought us back to Him and Him alone. God clearly showed us the difference between a visitation and permanent residency.

When we have a visitor come to our home, most of us change the sheets, dust, vacuum, and tidy up a bit. But when we have someone move in with us, there are usually major changes that take place. Now, you need to empty out the closet, remove your personal things from that room, and even possibly rearrangement the furniture a bit.

That is what happens in the spirit as well. As long as we only want a "guest" appearance from God, we don't need to make too many changes in our lifestyle. However, when we want Him to take up permanent residency and be the Lord over everything in our lives, we must allow the Holy Spirit to oversee the major changes.

 ## Time to Get Your Hiking Boots On

The God who made the world and everything in it is Lord of heaven and earth and does not live in temples built by hands.

(Acts 17:24 NIV)

Read Acts 17:24-27.

What is God looking for from us? _____

_____

Read 2 Corinthians 6:18.

What does God want us to be? _____

_____

Read 1 John 3:1.

What does God call us? _____

_____

What is the difference in a visitation and the permanent residency of God in us? _____

_____

_____

Which relationship do you want to have with Father God? _____

Pray and thank God that He desires a relationship with you, His child, and invite Him to take up permanent residency in your life.

Lord, please open my heart that You may have all of Me the same way You have given me all of You. You hold nothing back from Your child. I freely give You every part of my life. Come, O Lord, and have Your way in my life. Come, O Lord, and make my heart Your dwelling place.

Day Twenty-Three

How Did It Get So Complicated?

*"Come to Me, all you who are weary and bur-
dened, and I will give you rest. Take My yoke
upon you and learn from Me, for I am gentle
and humble in heart, and you will find rest
for your souls. For My yoke is easy and My
burden is light."* (Matthew 11:28-30 NIV)

Did you ever get so frustrated that you just
couldn't keep your focus? Well, I had just about
had enough and I cried out to the Lord in total frus-
tration, "Church should not be this complicated!"

In the Acts of the Apostles, we find the early
Church ran into some of the same problems.

Now then, why do you try to test God by putting on the necks of the disciples a yoke that neither we nor our fathers have been able to bear? (Acts 15:10 NIV)

In the ministry we are to partner with God to be a vessel He can use to help change and build up lives with His Word and His love. Then how does it become so complicated? When things start to become too complex and too cluttered, we may find ourselves just "going through the motions." That is not the type of ministry Jesus exemplified for us. As a matter of fact, He told us not to let anyone put us under a yoke of slavery of any kind.

It is for freedom that Christ has set us free. Stand firm, then, and do not let yourselves be burdened again by a yoke of slavery. (Galatians 5:1 NIV)

Then the Holy Spirit spoke to me, *"You are too busy with the ministry of the Lord that you neglect the Lord of the ministry."*

It was time to take a good look at the old "to do" list and get it uncomplicated. I remember the old saying, Keep It Simple Stupid—KISS! When I look at my personal "to do" list, it looks like I need several KISSES to come my way.

 ## Time to Get Your Hiking Boots On

Read our key verse for today from the Amplified translation of the Bible.

> *Come to Me, all you who labor and are heavy-laden and overburdened, and I will cause you to rest. [I will ease and relieve and refresh your souls.] Take My yoke upon you and learn of Me, for I am gentle (meek) and humble (lowly) in heart, and you will find rest (relief and ease and refreshment and recreation and blessed quiet) for your souls. For My yoke is wholesome (useful, good—not harsh, hard, sharp, or pressing, but comfortable, gracious, and pleasant), and My burden is light and easy to be borne.*
> (Matthew 11:28-30 AMP)

Have you ever felt heavy-laden and overburdened by your ministry commitments? _____

What did Jesus invite us to do if we are feeling this way? _____

Jesus says His yoke of ministry is useful, good, comfortable, gracious, and pleasant. It is not to be

_____

_____

Read Galatians 5:1. Whose job is it to keep us from putting on the yoke of slavery? _____

Take the time to review your ministry "to do" list. Ask God if He has given that task to you or if it is for another. A pastor once told me that if I am picking up a task that belongs to another, I am actually stealing their blessing.

As you pray today, ask the Holy Spirit to reveal any ministry task that you should put down. If you feel it is a heavy burden, chances are it is not yours to carry.

> *I thank you, Lord, for Your love and peace. Please help me, Lord, to know the ministry tasks that are mine and those that I need to lay down for another member of Your Body to do. I desire to be Your hands as I do my part of working within the Body of Christ.*

Day Twenty-Four

Where Is My GPS?

*Then Moses said, "If Your Presence does not
go with us, do not send us up from here."*
(Exodus 33:15a NIV)

It was time for a road trip and a little rest and relaxation. I began to check out the area and make my plans. One of my pet peeves is starting out on a trip without the directions. Somehow the shortcuts never end up being shorter. So, I do a MapQuest to get an idea as to how far away and how many hours it will take to get to our destination. Then I have to preview it on my GPS. Inevitably there is a bit of difference as to how MapQuest and the GPS say we should go. Both will probably get me there, but how do I determine which is the best way?

I think of the book of Exodus and wonder how I would have ever managed without having a GPS.

The trip would have made me a bit crazy. I can just hear myself asking Moses if he'd checked the map to make sure we weren't lost. We can laugh about that, but how many times do we take a trip in life and forget to turn on our spiritual GPS?

Moses knew how important it was to have God navigate his path and did not want to lead the people without God being with him. Exodus 33:12-17 lets us listen in on the dialogue between God and Moses as they discuss the journey to the Promised Land.

> *Moses said to the Lord, "You have been telling me, 'Lead these people,' but you have not let me know whom you will send with me. You have said, 'I know you by name and you have found favor with Me.' If You are pleased with me, teach me Your ways so I may know You and continue to find favor with You. Remember that this nation is Your people."*
>
> *The Lord replied, "My Presence will go with you, and I will give you rest."*
>
> *Then Moses said to Him, "If Your Presence does not go with us, do not send us up from here. How will anyone know that You are pleased with me and with Your people unless You go with us? What else will distinguish me and Your people on the face of the earth?"*
>
> *And the Lord said to Moses, "I will do the very thing you have asked, because I am pleased with you and I know you by name."*
>
> (NIV)

I believe God gave us this insight so we would understand the importance of seeking God's direction and presence in our lives so that we can safely reach our Promised Land.

 ## Time to Get Your Hiking Boots On

Many of the Old Testament writers knew the importance of having God's presence and direction in their lives. As you read the following Scriptures, ask the Holy Spirit to continually be your guide as you progress through your life's journey.

Record the insights the Holy Spirit gives from each of these verses.

Psalm 27:11 _____

_____

Psalm 61:1-2 _____

_____

Psalm 139:23-24 _____

_____

Psalm 143:10 _____

_____

Will you pray with me?

> *O Lord, I need You to go with me everywhere I go. Nothing can distinguish me from others except that Your Presence is with me. May I always be aware of Your Presence and the need for You to grant favor upon my life.*

Day Twenty-Five

Not Even a Hint

*But among you there must **not be even a hint** of sexual immorality, or of any kind of impurity, or of greed, because these are improper for God's holy people. Nor should there be obscenity, foolish talk or coarse joking, which are out of place, but rather thanksgiving. For of this you can be sure: No immoral, impure or greedy person—such a man is an idolater—has any inheritance in the kingdom of Christ and of God."* (Ephesians 5:3-4 NIV)

Before me I saw a bedroom. The dresser drawers where falling out and all the things inside the drawers were just shoved in, hanging out of each drawer. In the kitchen, the entire room was a mess, with food all over and trash on the floor. It was apparent the rooms were out of order. Things throughout the house had been left unattended. Cleanliness had apparently been left by the wayside. I asked the Lord what I was looking at.

I heard the Spirit of the Lord respond: *"Clean your house; clean your house."*

Our physical house may seem to be in order, but what about our spiritual house? Have you ever found yourself needing to move the plumb line of what you will allow yourself to be part of in order to fit in with friends, colleagues, and even family? Even in our Christian circles I have found that "off-color" joking is becoming more prominent than it was even just a few years ago. How can it be that in the presence of other God-fearing believers, I could possibly feel uncomfortable?

To me the words "clean your house" would mean to keep out even the little things that could eventually pile up and cause a big mess. Don't allow others to get your spiritual house dirty. Take the extra steps needed to guard your own spiritual dwelling. Proverbs 4:23-24 warns us to guard our hearts and our words.

Above all else, guard your heart, for it is the wellspring of life. Put away perversity from your mouth; keep corrupt talk far from your lips. (NIV)

 **Time to Get Your Hiking Boots On**

Read Proverbs 4:10-27.

List some of the warnings and advice given in this passage to help you keep your spiritual house clean.

Hold on to _____

Do not set foot on _____

Do not walk in _____

The wicked do not know _____

Above all guard _____

Put away _____

Keep corrupt _____

Read Philippians 4:8. What are the things we should be thinking and talking about? _____
_____
_____

I believe we all should pray this prayer every day so that we will keep our spiritual house in order:

Dear Lord, help me to honor You in all that I do, to keep watch over my spiritual dwelling, and not allow anything to come in that will displease or dishonor You. Let my house be Your dwelling place and bring You joy and honor. May the meditation of my heart and the words of my mouth bring You pleasure and honor.

Day Twenty-Six

What a Wonder

"For by Him all things were created: things in heaven and on earth, visible and invisible, whether thrones or powers or rulers or authorities; all things were created by Him and for Him." (Colossians 1:16 NIV)

Sitting on a beautiful beach, holding a glass of refreshing iced tea, and listening to the relaxing sound of the water can hardly be put into words. It had been a wonderful day of relaxing at the beach and watching families laughing and playing together. At the end of the day I was amazed to see how everyone stopped what they were doing to catch the beauty of the sunset. There was such a hush over the beach that I began to sing an old song.

Think with me...of the wonder of God! The galaxies! Creation! He has given us the gentle light of the moon to guide us at night and the powerful rays of the sun by day. The God of the universe, the Creator of heaven and earth, loves us unconditionally. What Grace!

It is so sobering to think that the same God, who is the Creator of the galaxies and the universe, takes the time to know all the little details about each one of us. He knows our struggles, hurts, and secrets. The God of the universe loves you and me!

Now most of us know we are to love and fear God, read the Bible, pray, worship God, and live out Christ in our lives, right? Well, I don't know about you, but at times this can be a challenge! It should be easy to love God, right? Could it be we have forgotten who God really is? Are we distracted because we are focused on what others have that we don't?

We must learn to intentionally push those negative thoughts aside and consistently remind ourselves of God's goodness. May every sunset remind us that we already have everything we need in Him. May we never lose the wonder of our amazing God!

 **Time to Get Your Hiking Boots On**

Read and meditate on these Scriptures written by the sweet psalmist. Bask in God's love and the wonder of His grace and mercy in your life.

Use these Psalms as your own prayer and declaration of the awesome wonder of our God.

> Psalm 47:2 – How _____ is the Lord Most High, great King over _____
>
> Psalm 66:5 – Come and see what God has done, how _____ His works in _____ behalf!
>
> Psalm 68:35 – You are _____ O God, in Your sanctuary; the God of Israel gives _____ and _____ to His people. Praise be to God!

Read Psalm 89:1-14.

List the words that the Psalmist uses to describe God and then also use them in your prayer for today.

_____ _____ _____

_____ _____ _____

Read Psalm 89:15-18.

List the benefits of walking in the light of God's presence given in these verses and thank God for His promises.

_____ _____ _____

May my thoughts of You, O God, never lose the awe of who You are. May You never become common to me. I am humbled to think that the God of the universe, the Creator of all things, desires to have fellowship with me. I love You, Lord, my God.

Day Twenty-Seven

Could I Be the One?

"I looked for a man among them who would build up the wall and stand before Me in the gap on behalf of the land so I would not have to destroy it, but I found none."

(Ezekiel 22:30 NIV)

With all that is going on in our nation and abroad, one would wonder what could possibility happen next? Most conversations are about our nation's leader; his skills, abilities, and the decisions he is making. One thing is for sure, it doesn't matter if you are building a building or a spiritual house—it will definitely require great wisdom.

During a time of worship and prayer, we began to intercede for the nation. The Scripture in Ezekiel 22 was the basis for our time of intercession. We felt it was time to humble ourselves and repent for the sins of our nation. One of our members, weeping before us, began to tell us how she was really tired of hearing all about our country's leadership and the way the nation was going, to the point she just didn't care anymore.

The Holy Spirit spoke to her heart saying, *"Pray for your nation. Because of David, I did not destroy Judah completely but left a remnant. Abraham asked Me to spare Sodom and Gorrmorah for ten righteous ones in that city. If I would have found the ten righteous, I would not have destroyed the city. Moses was only one man, but he brought down an entire empire. One person in prayer can make a difference."*

"If my people, who are called by My name, will humble themselves and pray and seek My face and turn from their wicked ways, then I will hear from heaven and will forgive their sin and heal their land."

(2 Chronicles 7:14 NIV)

In 2 Timothy 2:3-4 we read, "Endure hardship with us like a good soldier of Christ Jesus. No one serving as a soldier gets involved in civilian affairs—he wants to please his commanding officer" (NIV). Our Commander in Chief is Jesus Christ. We serve in the Lord's Army. Complaining will just cause us to stay in the desert a bit longer. So instead let's do what we are exhorted to do—pray for those in authority! The next time we find ourselves in a conversation where we are complaining or being discontent with all that is going on around us, let's lift up a prayer and be the ones that *stand in the gap.*

 ## Time to Get Your Hiking Boots On

Read Ezekiel 22:30.

What does it mean to stand *in the gap on behalf of the land*? _____

Read Psalm 106:23.

What would have happened if Moses had not stood in the gap? _____

Read 2 Chronicles 7:14.

What are the four things we need to do to have God forgive the sins of our nation and heal our land?

_____   _____

_____   _____

If it is your desire to be a good soldier in the Army of our Lord, then pray this prayer with me today and continue to pray for our nation and its leaders.

> *May I, O Lord, be the one to stand in the gap and intercede for this country and our leaders. Help me not to complain, but to bring this as a request before Your throne. Without You, we are nothing. Help us in our time of need.*

Day Twenty-Eight

Now That's a LOT of LOVING!

"A new command I give you: Love one another. As I have loved you, so you must love one another. By this all men will know that you are My disciples, if you love one another." (John 13:34-35 NIV)

Sitting at my desk, I began to ponder the significance of the Body of Christ. I was reminded of 1 Corinthians12:12-31 where God explained to us that we all are a part of His Body. We may all have different gifts and talents, come from different walks of life, and even attend different places of worship; yet we are equally important because Jesus Christ is our common foundation. Each person is like a different part of the Body with his or her own unique gifts to offer. When we begin to think we can do it alone, we are not only hurting ourselves, but we are hurting the Body of Christ. It would be like cutting off a finger or pulling out an eye, because we need each other.

We need to show God's love and stop the fighting among ourselves. Could I go as far as to say, when we fight against one another, we are fighting against Christ? We are so strongly advised in Galatians 5:15, "If you keep on biting and devouring each other, watch out or you will be destroyed by each other" (NIV). We are to serve and love one another.

Most of us could quote Scriptures on salvation, healing, blessings, promises, and finances; but how many times have we really meditated on Matthew 22:37-39? "Love the Lord your God with all your heart and with all your soul and with all your mind. This is the first and greatest commandment. And the second is like it: 'Love your neighbor as yourself'" (NIV).

Maybe it is time to repair some of our foundational cracks and go back to the basics. After all, John 17:20 records how Jesus prayed for us before He ascended into heaven, "that all of them may be one, Father, just as You are in Me and I am in You."

John 13:34-35 says, "A new command I give you: Love one another. As I have loved you, so you must love one another. By this all men will know that you are My disciples, if you love one another" (NIV). Now, that's a lot of loving!!!

 **Time to Get Your Hiking Boots On**

Read Galatians 5:15.

Define backbiting and strife. _____

_____

What do they do to the Body of Christ? _____

_____

Read Romans 12:18.

What does this verse admonish us to do? _____

_____

Read 1 Corinthians 1:10-13.

What does the Apostle Paul say about divisions in the Church? _____

Read 2 Timothy 2:14.

What does Paul advise Timothy to do to help keep division out of the Church? _____

Read John 13:34-35.

What has Jesus commanded us to do? _____
_____

Why? _____
_____

Pray and ask God to forgive you if you have been a cause for division in the Body of Christ. Then ask the Holy Spirit to guide you in showing God's love—first to the brethren and then to the world.

Day Twenty-Nine

Magnets—
the Power to Draw!

*"But I, when I am lifted up from the earth,
will draw all men to myself."*
(John 12:32 NIV)

One thing is for sure, when I see a sign that says
FREE or *CLEARANCE,* I am right there check-
ing out the situation. It is the type of magnet that will
draw me right to it. I think as Christians, we too have
a magnet. We have been drawn to Jesus and then we
are to draw others to Him.

What has drawn us to Jesus? Jesus answered this
very question in John 6:44. "No one can come to Me
unless the Father who sent Me draws him, and I will
raise him on the last day" (NIV).

In the Book of Hebrews, the Apostle Paul also
speaks about the importance of drawing near to God

so that we may encourage one another to persevere through trials.

> *Let us all come forward and* **draw near with true (honest and sincere) hearts in unqualified assurance and absolute conviction engendered by faith (by that leaning of the entire human personality on God in absolute trust and confidence in His power, wisdom, and goodness), having our hearts sprinkled and purified from a guilty (evil) conscience and our bodies cleansed with pure water.** *So let us seize and hold fast and retain without wavering the hope we cherish and confess and our acknowledgement of it, for He Who promised is reliable (sure) and faithful to His word. And let us consider and give attentive, continuous care to watching over one another, studying how we may stir up (stimulate and incite) to love and helpful deeds and noble activities, not forsaking or neglecting to assemble together [as believers], as is the habit of some people, but admonishing (warning, urging, and encouraging) one another, and all the more faithfully as you see the day approaching.* (Hebrews 10:22-25 AMP)

In the midst of preparing for a new study, my attention was drawn to the hours just before the death of Jesus. In His time of need, His friends scattered, and one even betrayed Him. Could it be that the lack of unity and love among Christians is somehow blocking the magnetic draw of Jesus in our lives? My prayer is that believers in Jesus Christ will be united in love for one another and that unbelievers will truly see Christ through this love.

If we build walls to protect ourselves from past wounds or possible hurt in our lives, they will prohibit our magnets from attracting others to the agape love of Christ. Jesus told His disciples in Matthew 10:8, "Freely you have received, freely give." When we do this we will be the magnets that draw the unsaved, hurting world to His salvation and His love.

We love because He first loved us.
(1 John 4:19 NIV)

Time to Get Your Hiking Boots On

Think back to when the Father drew you to Jesus. What were the circumstances in your life at the time? Briefly describe your experience. _____

_____

_____

_____

_____

_____

We always need to be ready to share our testimony with others. If you have never done so, write out your testimony and "rehearse" it so you can present it in three minutes or less.

God will send those our way that will be drawn to the testimony we have to share. Always be on the lookout for divine appointments. You may want to begin to journal all that the Lord is doing in your life so you can continually update your personal testimony.

As you prepare yourself to be a magnet to draw others to Jesus Christ, ask the Lord to help you always draw close to Him so that others will see His Spirit in you. Pray that His love will be magnified in your life to reflect the One you love and serve.

Day Thirty

Wait for the Gift

But very truly I tell you, *it is for your good* that I am going away. Unless I go away, the Advocate will not come to you; but if I go, *I will send him to you.* When he comes, he will prove the world to be in the wrong about sin and righteousness and judgment. *I have much more to say to you, more than you can now bear. But when he, the Spirit of truth, comes, he will guide you into all the truth. He will not speak on his own; he will speak only what he hears, and he will tell you what is yet to come. He will glorify me because it is from me that he will receive what he will make known to you. All that belongs to the Father is mine. That is why I said the Spirit will receive from me what he will make known to you."*

(John 16:7, 8, 12-14 NIV)

What better teacher could the disciples have had then Jesus? Yet He tells them He must go so that the Holy Spirit, "whom the Father will send in My name, will teach you all things and will remind you of everything I have said to you" (John 14:26 NIV). With all the teaching and all the discipleship they received from Jesus, He told them He would still send something greater.

I wrote about all that Jesus began to do and to teach until the day he was taken up to heaven, after giving instructions through the Holy Spirit to the apostles he had chosen. After his suffering, he presented himself to them and gave many convincing proofs that he was alive. He appeared to them over a period of forty days and spoke about the kingdom of God.

*On one occasion, while he was eating with them, he gave them this command: "**Do not leave Jerusalem, but wait for the gift my Father promised,** which you have heard me speak about. For John baptized with water, but in a few days you will be baptized with the Holy Spirit".*

Then they gathered around him and asked him, "Lord, are you at this time going to restore the kingdom to Israel?"

He said to them: "It is not for you to know the times or dates the Father has set by his own authority. But you will receive power when the Holy Spirit comes on you; and you will be my witnesses in Jerusalem, and in all Judea and Samaria, and to the ends of the earth." (Acts 1:1-8 NIV)

Wait; He told them to wait! This is not one of my favorite words. My mind is thinking: my Lord has risen from the dead, He appeared to the apostles, He spoke to them about the Kingdom of God, and now He commands them to wait? At this point, I think I would have been out the door telling everyone what had just happened!

Jesus knew they needed the Holy Spirit and His power in order to go and fulfill their great commission. Peter had fallen asleep when it was a time to pray, then he denied Jesus in the garden three times. Yet after he was filled with the Holy Spirit, he preached to the crowd with such boldness that, "when the people heard this, they were *cut to the heart* and said to Peter and the other apostles, 'Brothers, what shall we do?'" (Acts 2:37 NIV). What boldness and transformation!

We can look at Peter and John, filled with the Holy Spirit in Acts 4:13, as they spoke to the rulers and elders. "When they saw the courage of Peter and John and realized that they were *unschooled, ordinary men*, they were *astonished* and they took note that these men had been with Jesus" (NIV).

Then we could look at Stephen in Acts 6:8, "Now Stephen, a man full of God's grace and power, performed great wonders and signs among the people. Opposition arose, however, from members of the Synagogue of the Freedmen (as it was called) — Jews of Cyrene and Alexandria, as well as the provinces of Cilicia and Asia—who began to argue with Stephen. But *they could not stand up against the wisdom the Spirit gave him as he spoke"* (NIV).

Change will take place when the Word of God is preached in the power and love of the Holy Spirit.

Paul also knew he needed the power of the Holy Spirit. "My message and my preaching were not with wise and persuasive words, but with a demonstration of the Spirit's power, so that your faith might not rest on human wisdom, but on God's power" (1 Corinthians 2:4,5 NIV).

Let me share something I read from E. M. Bounds, a Methodist minister of a hundred years ago.

> *The power of Christ's dispensation is a fiery pulpit—not a learned pulpit, not a popular pulpit, not an eloquent pulpit, but a pulpit on fire with the Holy Ghost...*
>
> *This power is not the mere iteration or reiteration of truth well learned or well told, but it is the enabling force to declare revealed truth with superhuman authority. The preacher must have the power given by direct connection with God...*
>
> *God does not mix this power with other solutions to give it efficiency. It is not some or much of the Holy Ghost mixed with some or much of other ingredients. This power is from the Holy Ghost singular and alone. It is the one thing to be sought and secured, the one thing whose importance discredits all other*

things, the one thing that stands alone unri-
valed and supreme.
(E. M. Bounds, *Powerful and Prayerful
Pulpits,* Grand Rapids: Baker, 1993. p. 43)

Preaching is not how eloquent you are or how wise you may be; what makes a change is the power of the Holy Spirit. When Peter preached, they were cut to the heart; their heart was humbled and broken.

Evangelist D. L. Moody's heart became increasingly concerned over the years as he saw spiritual decline in so many churches. How could he effectively extend God's Kingdom if the local congregations were lukewarm? Toward the end of the nineteenth century he called a special convocation for prayer and waiting upon the Lord for "a new enduement of power from on high." His talks were condensed into a book published under the title, *Secret Power.*

There has been much inquiry of late of the Holy Spirit. In this and other lands, thousands of persons have been giving attention to the study of this grand theme. I hope it will lead us all to pray for a greater manifestation of His power upon the whole church of God.

How much we have dishonored Him in the past! How ignorant of His Grace and Love and Presence we have been! True, we have heard of Him and read of Him, but we have had little intelligent knowledge of His attributes, His offices, and His relations to us...

Let others reject, if they will, at their own peril, this imperishable truth. I believe, and am growing more into this belief, that divine, miraculous, creative power resides in the Holy Spirit...

Unless He attend the word in power, vain will be the attempt in preaching it. Human eloquence or persuasiveness of speech are the mere trappings of the dead. If the living Spirit be absent, the prophet may preach to the bones in the valley, but it must be the breath from heaven that will cause the slain to live...

If we want that power to quicken our friends who are dead in sin, we must look to God, and not be looking to man to do it. If we look alone to ministers, if we look alone to Christ's disciples to do this work, we shall be disappointed. If we look to the Spirit of God and expect it to come from Him and Him alone, then we shall honor the Spirit, and the Spirit will do His work.

I cannot help but believe that there are many Christians who want to be more efficient in the Lord's service. It is from the Holy Spirit that we many expect this power.

Dwight L Moody, *Secret Power*
(Chicago: Moody, 1881)[1]

[1] ***Fresh Power*** by Jim Cymbala with Dean Merrill (Zondervan) Copyright © 2001 by Jim Cymbala, The Library of Congress has catalogued the original hardcover edition as follows: Cymbala, Jim 1943- Fresh power: experiencing the vast resources of the Spirit of God / Jim Cymbala with Dean Merrill. He quotes D. L. Moody in a Prologue and Bounds in Chapter 4.

The Lord showed me the "dry bones" of Ezekiel 37:4-5 as the Church today, corporately and individually. Even when people are leaving church, they are downcast with no joy and no life.

Prophesy to these bones and say to them, "Dry bones, hear the word of the LORD! This is what the Sovereign LORD says to these bones: I will make breath enter you, and you will come to life." (Ezekiel 37:4-5 NIV)

If our spiritual and physical life has become mundane, it is caused by not allowing the Holy Spirit to come and bring life. We blame the church, but as individuals, we can be the one to have a "flicker" and be a light in this darkness to bring back life, both individually and corporately. The Holy Spirit is here waiting for us to welcome Him back home.

 ## Time to Get Your Hiking Boots On

As children of God, we need to become familiar with the work of the Holy Spirit. Read the following verses and record what you learn about this third member of the Trinity.

John 14:26 says the Holy Spirit will _____
_____

John 16:13 says the Holy Spirit will _____
_____

Romans 8:9 warns us that if we do not have the Holy Spirit, then _____

Romans 8:26 says the Holy Spirit helps us _____
_____

Galatians 5:22-23 gives us the _____
_____

Read again Acts 1:1-8. In your own words explain what you believe the Holy Spirit will do in your life:
_____
_____
_____
_____
_____

Have you ever felt discouraged, disappointed, and in need of a refreshing drink, physically or spiritually? Where has our joy gone? When all of this overwhelms me, I stop and wait for the living water of the Holy Spirit and let fresh breath enter in and bring life.

Dear Holy Spirit, I know You are waiting for us to welcome You back home. Please forgive us for ignoring You and not allowing You to do the work You have been sent to do. Please come and fill us, guide us, and empower us. Please give us fresh breath from heaven and cause us to be alive once again. Please take the worries of the world that surround us and fill us with Your peace and joy to overflowing. Let us be that light that will shine ever so bright.

Conclusion

The Free Gift of God

When we read the Bible, we see that God created all things. Adam had no sin, but he made a choice to disobey God's command, and this caused a separation from God, resulting in spiritual death. The Bible tells us in Romans 3:23 that we all have sinned. Before God sent Adam and Eve from the Garden, He made a promise to send a deliverer—His name would be Jesus.

Jesus left His place in heaven and became a man in order to give Himself as an offering for sin. His death on the cross took the judgment of our sin to free us. When we receive Jesus Christ as our personal Lord and Savior, we die to ourselves and are spiritually reborn.

For if you confess with your mouth that Jesus is Lord and believe in your heart that God raised Him from the dead, you will be saved. For it is by believing in your heart that you are made right with God, and it is by confessing with your mouth that you are saved."

(Romans 10:9-10 NLT)

We are not saved by our good works or deeds. We are saved by His grace. It is a free gift that we cannot earn. If you believe Christ died for you and you are willing to give Him your life and no longer live for yourself, then you are ready to pray and become a child of God. Perhaps you have tasted the Lord in your life and you walked away from Him and you are ready to come back home. Then you, too, are ready to pray and have a right standing with God.

If that is where you are today, pray this prayer with me:

Father God, I come before You right now, knowing that I am a sinner. I am thankful to You for sending Your Son, Jesus, to die for my sins on the cross. I ask You to forgive me for all the sins that I have committed and the ways I have displeased You. Thank Your for Your gift of salvation and Your Grace towards me. I give You my life. Jesus, I confess You as my Lord and my Savior. Please come into my life through Your Spirit and change me into Your child. I will no longer live for myself, but will live for You. Lord Jesus, guide me through this journey here on earth and keep me close to You. My life is completely in Your hands. Amen

About the Author

A lice married her best friend, Ed, in 1973. They have three amazing children: Eddie, Michelle, and David. They also have three beautiful grandchildren: Moriah, Declan, Hannah, and Jude Kingsley. Their lives have been truly blessed by the hand of God.

God's grace and love drew her heart to a relationship with her Lord and Savior Jesus Christ in 1980. Her earthy journey has become one of excitement, perseverance, and trusting in God.